Fibonnaci Fun

Fascinating Activities with Intriguing Numbers

Trudi Hammel Garland

DALE SEYMOUR PUBLICATIONS ®

Acknowledgments

I wish to thank Kaye Kramer for inspiring this collection of activities with a Fibonacci focus. I appreciate the opinions offered by Judith Kennedy and Carey Carpenter, and I am deeply indebted to Catherine Epstein and Hillary Hoppock for their time and expertise. I will always be grateful for the loving encouragement of Bruce Garland.

Project Editor: Joan Gideon

Production Coordinator: Shannon Miller

Illustrative Art: Rachel Gage

Technical Art: Shirley Bortoli

Text and cover Design: Nancy Benedict

Published by Dale Seymour Publications®, an imprint of the Alternative Publishing Group of Addison-Wesley Publishing Company.

Order number DS21804

ISBN 1-57232-265-9

2 3 4 5 6 7 8 9 10-ML-00 99 98 97

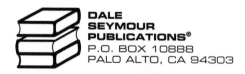

DALE
SEYMOUR
PUBLICATIONS®
P.O. BOX 10888
PALO ALTO, CA 94303

Contents

Connections Chart

	1	2	3	4	5	6	7	8	9	10	11	12	13	14	15	16	17	18	19	20	21	P1	P2	P3
Algebra			×														×			×	×	×	×	
Art												×										×	×	
Binary Numbers																		×						
Calculator											×			×					×					
Coordinate Geometry									×															
Geometry													×		×	×	×						×	
Math History							×	×												×	×			
Life Science									×	×														×
Logic	×			×	×	×	×	×		×	×									×	×			
Measurement																							×	
Networks				×																				
Order of Operations																			×					
Patterns	×		×	×	×	×	×	×	×	×	×			×										
Problem Solving				×	×	×	×	×												×	×			
Proportion												×										×	×	
Sequences	×	×																						
Statistics																						×	×	
Visual Thinking															×	×	×							

How to Use This Book

This book contains more than 25 classroom activities featuring Fibonacci numbers and the golden ratio. Use them to teach or to reinforce many mathematical topics, connecting the topics with a common, intriguing thread. The activities are generally grouped by topic and generally presented in order of difficulty. Since many activities have the same connections and classes vary in ability, you should examine each activity to choose those that meet your students' needs.

Of each two-page spread, one page is a blackline master for the student. It is a self-contained activity with directions, questions, and additional information. Each group of students needs one copy of the activity unless otherwise indicated in the teacher notes.

The opposite page is addressed to you, the teacher. It includes

- connections to other topics
- a list of materials needed
- grouping suggestions
- estimated time required
- notes
- alerts or cautions
- extensions for advanced students
- answers
- references to these publications

Garland, Trudi Hammel. *Fascinating Fibonaccis: Mystery and Magic in Numbers.* Palo Alto, California: Dale Seymour Publications, 1987.

Runion, Garth E. *The Golden Section.* Palo Alto, California: Dale Seymour Publications, 1990.

These materials are designed for grades 5 to 8. The suggested grouping and estimated time requirement can vary widely. Review the activity to determine what grouping and duration are appropriate for your students. Use these activities for the entire class as

- an extended unit on Fibonacci numbers and the golden ratio
- separate activities to be used when time or circumstances permit
- fun Fibonacci days before vacation or at the end of the year
- constructive use of a day with a substitute teacher

You may also use these activities for individualized instruction as

- enrichment for any student any time
- packets of activities for high-achieving students to work on independently
- extensions of specific topics for students who complete their work early

Some activities are field studies or projects you could extend over time. These connect math to the real world and provide hands-on opportunities for open-ended investigations.

Students could gather these activities together in notebooks, journals, or portfolios as a source of reference.

What are Fibonacci Numbers?

Fibonacci numbers make up the Fibonacci sequence named after a medieval mathematician, Leonardo of Pisa, son of Bonacci. He established the sequence of numbers around A.D. 1200 to answer a problem about the breeding of rabbits: How many pairs of rabbits would be in a pen after 12 months if you start with a pair of adult rabbits who have a pair of babies at the first of each month. All baby rabbits take one month to become adults and bear a pair of baby rabbits at the first of each month, forever—no rabbits die. The number of pairs in the pen through the years follows the Fibonacci sequence.

The first, simplest, and smallest Fibonacci number is 1.   **1**

The sequence is built by adding two numbers together and getting the next number. If the only number so far (1) is added to no number before it (0), another 1 will result.   **1**

Now, there are two numbers that can be added together to produce the next number.   **2**

Adding the last two numbers in the sequence produces the next number.   **3**

Each number is the sum of the previous two numbers.   **5**

These are the Fibonacci numbers.   **8**

The sequence can continue forever.   **13**

There is an infinite number of entries in the sequence.   **21**

This is no ordinary sequence of numbers, however.   **34**

The numbers appear in many diverse places such as nature, art, architecture, music, poetry, astronomy, computer science, psychology, gambling, chemistry, the human body, physics, and the stock market. You simply have to know how to find them!   **55**   **89**

The mathematical relationships of Fibonacci numbers are intriguing. For example, consider the following:

- The product of any two alternating Fibonacci number differs from the square of the middle number in the sequence by 1:
  ($8 \times 21 = 168$; $13^2 = 169$).

- The difference between the squares of any two alternating Fibonacci numbers is a Fibonacci number:
  $5^2 = 25$ and $13^2 = 169$; $169 - 25 = 144$.

What Is the Golden Ratio?

The *golden ratio* is a relationship that exists between two dimensions characterized by unique mathematical properties and especially pleasing visual balance. This ratio is found in the dimensions of a golden rectangle.

The *golden cut* is that division of a line segment into two unequal but visually harmonious segments that bear the following relationship:

$$\frac{\text{Small Part}}{\text{Large Part}} = \frac{\text{Large Part}}{\text{Entire Length}}$$

or

$$\frac{AB}{BC} = \frac{BC}{AC}$$

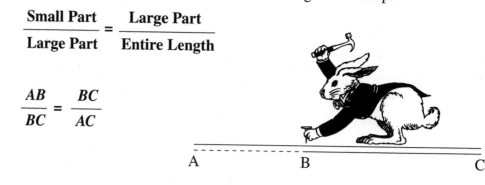

A   B   C

One of the many interesting properties of the golden rectangle is that if you remove a square from it, the remaining rectangle is similar to the original.

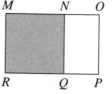

QNOP has the same proportions as *MOPR*; it is simply smaller.

The golden ratio can be expressed either as $\frac{0.618\ldots}{1}$ or $\frac{1}{1.618\ldots}$ depending on whether the small or large part is designated to be 1.

The irrational numbers 0.618. . . and 1.618. . . are unique—they are each others' reciprocals ± 1. This is true for no other pair of numbers.

What Do Fibonacci Numbers Have to Do with the Golden Ratio?

Ratios of consecutive Fibonacci numbers come very close to the golden ratio.

- After the first number, any Fibonacci number divided by the next larger one will produce a number smaller than 1.

- After the first number, any Fibonacci number divided by the previous one will produce a number larger than 1.

- The further along in the sequence the numbers are, the closer the ratios get to the golden ratio (0.618. . . or 1.618. . .), ultimately accurate to an infinite number of decimal places!

Fibonacci Number	Ratios Smaller Than 1		Ratios Larger Than 1	
5	$\frac{5}{8}$	0.625000	$\frac{5}{3}$	1.666667
8	$\frac{8}{13}$	0.615385	$\frac{8}{5}$	1.600000
13	$\frac{13}{21}$	0.619048	$\frac{13}{8}$	1.625000
21	$\frac{21}{34}$	0.617647	$\frac{21}{13}$	1.615385
34	$\frac{34}{55}$	0.618182	$\frac{34}{21}$	1.619048
55	$\frac{55}{89}$	0.617978	$\frac{55}{34}$	1.617647
89	$\frac{89}{144}$	0.618056	$\frac{89}{55}$	1.618182
144	$\frac{144}{233}$	0.618026	$\frac{144}{89}$	1.617978
233	$\frac{233}{377}$	0.618037	$\frac{233}{144}$	1.618056

Because of this relationship, large Fibonacci numbers can be used to achieve the golden ratio.

Artists and designers may use Fibonacci numbers as a simple means to achieve a visually pleasing balance in their work. Musicians and architects do the same thing— sometimes knowingly, but not always. Beautiful pieces of music and art have been analyzed and found to divide into Fibonacci numbers! This is especially true for art found in nature.

The First 50 Fibonacci Numbers

1.	1	26.	121,393
2.	1	27.	196,418
3.	2	28.	317,811
4.	3	29.	514,229
5.	5	30.	832,040
6.	8	31.	1,346,269
7.	13	32.	2,178,309
8.	21	33.	3,524,578
9.	34	34.	5,702,887
10.	55	35.	9,227,465
11.	89	36.	14,930,352
12.	144	37.	24,157,817
13.	233	38.	39,088,169
14.	377	39.	63,245,986
15.	610	40.	102,334,155
16.	987	41.	165,580,141
17.	1,597	42.	267,914,296
18.	2,584	43.	433,494,437
19.	4,181	44.	701,408,733
20.	6,765	45.	1,134,903,170
21.	10,946	46.	1,836,311,903
22.	17,711	47.	2,971,215,073
23.	28,657	48.	4,807,526,976
24.	46,368	49.	7,778,742,049
25.	75,025	50.	12,586,269,025

Activities

Fibonacci Figuring

CONNECTIONS	sequences • patterns
MATERIALS	copy of Activity 1 • calculator
GROUPING	1 to 3
DURATION	20 minutes
NOTES	Calculators are optional. The activity requires only simple addition.

When students list the numbers in order, the numbers constitute the *Fibonacci sequence*—an infinite sequence of numbers generated recursively, the next number determined by operation on numbers already in the sequence. Any sequence of numbers generated by the rule "each number is the sum of the previous two" is referred to as a Fibonacci-type sequence.

The numbers are named after the medieval mathematician Leonardo of Pisa (ca. 1180–1250) who wrote under the pen name Fibonacci. He first established the sequence in his famous book *Liber Abaci* by giving the solution to a math problem about breeding rabbits. The numbers are fascinating in varied contexts—especially mathematically and geometrically. (See "What Are Fibonacci Numbers?" page 7.)

Check students extended lists of Fibonacci numbers against the list of the first 50 Fibonacci numbers on page 10. *Fascinating Fibonaccis* gives the first 100 Fibonacci numbers.

ALERT!	Students should be careful getting started. They begin with two 1s.
EXTENSIONS	• Memorize the first 12 or 15 Fibonacci numbers. Be familiar enough with them to recognize them readily.
	• Examine an extended list of self-generated Fibonacci numbers for interesting patterns and relationships.
	• Prime factor the Fibonacci numbers and look for patterns and relationships.
MORE INFORMATION	*Fascinating Fibonaccis,* chapter 1 and chapter 7. There are lots of interesting patterns and relationships here.
ANSWERS	**List:** 8; 13; 21; 34; 55; 89; 144; 233; 377; 610; 987; 1,597; 2,584

1. 5; it is the same number   **2.** 144; it is the square of 12 or 12^2

3. an infinite number   **4.** 2 to 1

5. 75,025

NAME _____

Fibonacci Figuring

Eight hundred years ago there lived a mathematician Leonardo of Pisa, who was called Fibonacci because he was the son of Bonacci. He was the first person to write down an important list of numbers that has since been named for him. You can easily construct his list of numbers.

This is the rule:

Each number is the sum of the previous two numbers in the list.

- Begin with the number 1, the most basic of all numbers.

- Add that first number (1) to the previous number in the list (in this case zero, since there is no previous number).

- Add the previous two numbers to get the next number.

- Add the previous two numbers to get the next number.

- To continue, create each number by adding the previous two numbers.

List

	1
$1 + 0 = 1$	**1**
$1 + 1 = 2$	**2**
$2 + 1 = 3$	_____
	_____
	_____

The numbers in this list are the *Fibonacci numbers*.

When they are listed in this order, they are the *Fibonacci sequence*.

After you reach the bottom of this sheet, continue the Fibonacci sequence as long as you like on the back. Look at your numbers and find interesting patterns and relationships. Then, answer these questions.

1. What is the 5th Fibonacci number? _____

    What is interesting about this?

2. What is the 12th Fibonacci number? _____

    What is interesting about this?

3. How many Fibonacci numbers are there? _____

4. What seems to be the ration of odd Fibonacci numbers to even Fibonacci numbers?

5. What is the 25th Fibonacci number? _____

Sorting Sequences

CONNECTIONS	sequences • patterns • logic
MATERIALS	copy of Activity 2 • calculator
GROUPING	1 to 3
DURATION	20 to 30 minutes
NOTES	This set of sequences includes

- arithmetic sequences where each number is the sum of a specific number and the previous number—for example, add 3 each time

- geometric sequences where each number is the product of a specific number and the previous number—for example, multiply by 3 each time

- power sequences where each number is a specific power of sequential numbers—for example, the third power of counting numbers

- recursive sequences where each number is a function of the preceding numbers, which change as the sequence progresses—for example, the Fibonacci sequence

ALERT! Question 24 is a popular puzzle. It is not a mathematical sequence, really. These are the first letters of the numbers one, two, three, four, and so on.

EXTENSIONS

- Find examples in the activity of each of the sequences identified in the Notes.

- Make up your own original set of sequences and see if others can continue them. You could use fractions, decimals, negative numbers, coordinate pairs, or other sequences.

MORE INFORMATION *Fascinating Fibonaccis,* chapter 7, pages 65–66

ANSWERS

1. 30, 35, 40	**2.** 44, 51, 58	**3.** 36, 33, 30	**4.** 70, 64, 58
5. 30, 42, 56	**6.** 19, 25, 32	**7.** 984, 978, 971	**8.** 56, 52, 50
9. 9, 14, 9	**10.** 29, 28, 38	**11.** 5, 4, 6	**12.** 366, 374, 324
13. 106, 148, 197	**14.** 110, 134, 162	**15.** 13, 21, 34	**16.** 243, 729, 2187
17. 29, 47, 76	**18.** 512; 2,048; 8,192	**19.** 6, 3, 1.5	**20.** 13, 20, 17
21. 36, 49, 64	**22.** 11,111; 111,111; 1,111,111		
23. 22, 35, 56	**24.** *N, T, E* (see Alert)		

Sorting Sequences

Find the next three entries in each of these sequences.

1.   5,   10,   15,   20,   25, _____ , _____ , _____

2.   9,   16,   23,   30,   37, _____ , _____ , _____

3.   51,   48,   45,   42,   39, _____ , _____ , _____

4.   100,   94,   88,   82,   76, _____ , _____ , _____

5.   0,   2,   6,   12,   20, _____ , _____ , _____

6.   4,   5,   7,   10,   14, _____ , _____ , _____

7.   999,   998,   996,   993,   989, _____ , _____ , _____

8.   70,   68,   64,   62,   58, _____ , _____ , _____

9.   14,   9,   14,   9,   14, _____ , _____ , _____

10.   1,   11,   10,   20,   19, _____ , _____ , _____

11.   1,   3,   2,   4,   3, _____ , _____ , _____

12.   500,   450,   458,   408,   416, _____ , _____ , _____

13.   1,   8,   22,   43,   71, _____ , _____ , _____

14.   50,   54,   62,   74,   90, _____ , _____ , _____

15.   1,   1,   2,   3,   5,   8, _____ , _____ , _____

16.   1,   3,   9,   27,   81, _____ , _____ , _____

17.   1,   3,   4,   7,   11,   18, _____ , _____ , _____

18.   2,   8,   32,   128, _____ , _____ , _____

19.   48,   24,   12, _____ , _____ , _____

20.   1,   8,   5,   12,   9,   16, _____ , _____ , _____

21.   1,   4,   9,   16,   25, _____ , _____ , _____

22.   1,   11,   111,   1111, _____ , _____ , _____

23.   2,   2,   3,   4,   6,   9,   14, _____ , _____ , _____

24.   O,   T,   T,   F,   F,   S,   S,   E, _____ , _____ , _____

TO THE TEACHER

Sum Fun!

CONNECTIONS	patterns
MATERIALS	copy of Activity 3
GROUPING	1 to 4
DURATION	15 minutes

NOTES
Encourage students to list the sums by beginning with the largest number in each case and working their way down. It helps them recognize the patterns. Writing numbers this way is called the Zeckendorf representation.

You could develop this into a contest. Give credit for speed and accuracy, but penalize errors or the use of adjacent Fibonacci numbers.

ALERT!
These are to be sums of non-adjacent Fibonacci numbers, though it is tempting to ignore this directive.

EXTENSIONS
• Investigate if any of these numbers can be written in more than one way using non-adjacent Fibonacci numbers.

• Using a table of Fibonacci numbers (see page 10 of this book), create large numbers as sums of large Fibonacci numbers.

MORE INFORMATION
Fascinating Fibonaccis, chapter 7, pages 65–78

ANSWERS

$6 = 5 + 1$	$22 = 21 + 1$	$41 = 34 + 5 + 2$
$9 = 8 + 1$	$23 = 21 + 2$	$42 = 34 + 8$
$10 = 8 + 2$	$24 = 21 + 3$	$43 = 34 + 8 + 1$
$11 = 8 + 3$	$25 = 21 + 3 + 1$	$44 = 34 + 8 + 2$
$12 = 8 + 3 + 1$	$26 = 21 + 5$	$45 = 34 + 8 + 3$
$14 = 13 + 1$	$27 = 21 + 5 + 1$	$47 = 34 + 13$
$15 = 13 + 2$	$28 = 21 + 5 + 2$	$48 = 34 + 13 + 1$
$16 = 13 + 3$	$29 = 21 + 8$	$49 = 34 + 13 + 2$
$17 = 13 + 3 + 1$	$30 = 21 + 8 + 1$	$50 = 34 + 13 + 3$
$19 = 13 + 5 + 1$	$31 = 21 + 8 + 2$	$60 = 55 + 5$
$20 = 13 + 5 + 2$	$33 = 21 + 8 + 3 + 1$	$70 = 55 + 13 + 2$
	$35 = 34 + 1$	$80 = 55 + 21 + 3 + 1$
	$36 = 34 + 2$	$100 = 89 + 8 + 3$
	$37 = 34 + 3$	$1000 = 987 + 13$
	$38 = 34 + 3 + 1$	
	$39 = 34 + 5$	

Sum Fun

The Fibonacci sequence is 1, 1, 2, 3, 5, 8, and so one. Each number is the sum of the previous two numbers. You can represent all positive integers either as a Fibonacci number or as the sum of non-adjacent (meaning "not next to each other in the sequence") Fibonacci numbers. Show the following integers represented this way. Some have been done for you.

List the Fibonacci numbers in the right column. Use this list to create sums that equal the integers. Do not use two numbers next to each other!

Fibonacci numbers

			1

Look for patterns!

1 = 1	21 = 21	41 =	**1**
2 = 2	22 =	42 =	**2**
3 = 3	23 =	43 =	**3**
4 = 3 + 1	24 =	44 =	**5**
5 = 5	25 =	45 =	
6 =	26 =	46 = 34 + 8 + 3 + 1	
7 = 5 + 2	27 =	47 =	
8 = 8	28 =	48 =	
9 =	29 =	49 =	
10 =	30 =	50 =	
11 =	31 =		
12 =	32 = 21 + 8 + 3	60 =	
13 = 13	33 =		
14 =	34 = 34	70 =	
15 =	35 =		
16 =	36 =	80 =	
17 =	37 =		
18 = 13 + 5	38 =	100 =	
19 =	39 =		
20 =	40 = 34 + 5 + 1	1000 =	

Crawling Critters

CONNECTIONS	networks • problem solving • patterns
MATERIALS	copy of Activity 4 • set of colored pencils or pens • copy of Supplement 1 (for Extensions) • chalk and chalkboard (for Extensions)
GROUPING	1 to 3
DURATION	15 to 25 minutes

NOTES

Encourage students to do this network problem by simply adding together the number of ways to get to the intersections immediately preceding the intersection in question. For example, if there are 3 ways to get to intersection *D* and 5 ways to get to intersection E, then there will then be 8 ways to get to *F* since the only access is through *D* or *E*.

The colored pencils particularly help younger students sketch the paths. They are optional for older students.

ALERT!

The ant never backtracks. It does not matter how slowly the ant progresses, as long as it never goes in the opposite direction, even slightly!

EXTENSIONS

• For fun, sketch all 13 paths from *A* to *G* or all 21 paths from *A* to *H*. The sheet of mazes on page 66 will accommodate all 34 paths from *A* to *I*.

• *Sprouts* is a simple game of networks. Divide into two teams. Begin with any number of points, such as 5. A team makes a play by connecting any two points on the board with a line (straight or curvy) and creating a new point on the line. That new point can be used like the others. Teams alternate making plays.

There are two rules:

1. Point is *used up* if three lines come into it. It cannot be connected again.

2. No existing line can be crossed with a new line.

The team that makes the last connection wins, or the first team that can make no more connections loses.

MORE INFORMATION *Fascinating Fibonaccis,* chapter 6, pages 55, 56

ANSWERS

1. 1   **2.** 2   **3.** 3   **4.** 5

5. 8 sketches (one maze will be empty since there are only 8 paths)

6. 21   **7.** 233   **8.** 121,393   **9.** yes, Fibonacci numbers

NAME _____

Crawling Critters

An ant is trying to crawl through this alphabetical maze of tunnels.

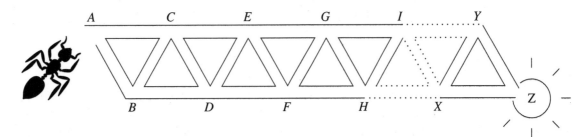

It starts at *A* and always moves in the general direction of its goal *Z* (left to right), never going even slightly backward (right to left).

How many different paths might the ant take going from

1. *A* to *B*? _____   **2.** *A* to *C*? _____   **3.** *A* to *D*? _____

4. *A* to *E*? _____   **5.** *A* to *F*? _____

Below, sketch as many paths from *A* to *F* as you can find.

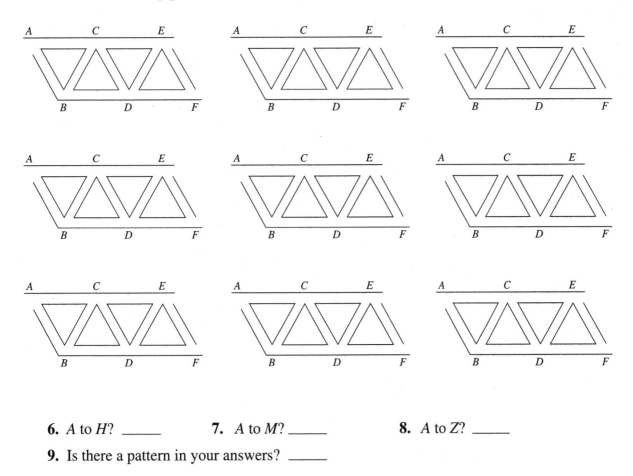

6. *A* to *H*? _____   **7.** *A* to *M*? _____   **8.** *A* to *Z*? _____

9. Is there a pattern in your answers? _____

TO THE TEACHER

Boy Bees

CONNECTIONS	life science • problem solving • patterns
MATERIALS	copy of Activity 5
GROUPING	2 to 4
DURATION	15 minutes
NOTES	In contrast to Fibonacci's famous contrived problem about the rabbits, bees really do breed as described in this problem. The female bee is the queen bee, and the only one to develop from a fertilized egg.
ALERT!	As students work up the bee's family tree, they should put lots of space between the symbols *M* and *F* to leave room for the next generations' *M*s and *F*s.
EXTENSION	Investigate bee reproduction and report back to the class.
MORE INFORMATION	*Fascinating Fibonaccis,* chapter 2, page 13
ANSWERS	

Generations Back		M	F	Total
9		21	34	55
8		13	21	34
7	**and so on**	8	13	21
6	M F F M F M F F M F F M F	5	8	13
5	F M F F M F M F	3	5	8
4	M F F M F	2	3	5
3	F M F	1	2	3
2	M F	1	1	2
1	F	0	1	1

Male Bee

NAME _____

Boy Bees

Find the family tree for male bees using these simple rules:

- Male bees have only one parent—a female. (They develop from unfertilized eggs.)

- Female bees have two parents—a male and female.

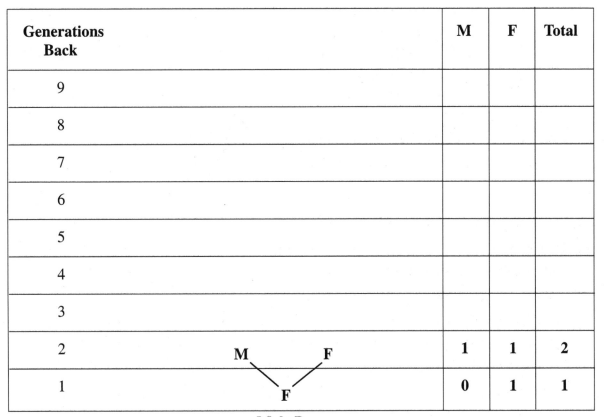

Generations Back		M	F	Total
9				
8				
7				
6				
5				
4				
3				
2	M F	1	1	2
1	F	0	1	1

Male Bee

Family tree begins here.

(Work from the bottom up.)

Complete the chart by indicating the number of ancestors the male bee has in each generation back.

Remember, the generation preceding each male will show only a female parent for that male; the generation preceding each female will show both a female and male parent for that female.

ACTIVITY

6

TO THE TEACHER

Tallying Tokens

CONNECTIONS	logic • problem solving • patterns
MATERIALS	copy of Activity 6
GROUPING	1 to 3
DURATION	20 minutes
NOTES	Students need to use a logical, orderly approach when listing the configurations of *N*s and *D*s.
ALERT!	At first it appears there are as many ways to pay for these tokens as there are numbers of tokens. But students looking for a pattern will discover there are 5 ways to pay for 4 tokens, and from then on, the numbers are not equal.
EXTENSION	Use an orderly list to find the 55 ways to pay for 9 tokens
MORE INFORMATION	*Fascinating Fibonaccis,* chapter 6, pages 53, 54

ANSWERS

4. (NNNN), (DD), (NDN), (DNN), (NND)   5

5. (DNNN), (DDN), (NDNN), (NNND), (NNDN), (DND), (NDD), (NNNNN)   8

6. (NNNNNN), (DDNN), (DNDN), (NDND), (NNNND), (NNNDN), (NNDNN),
   (NDNNN), (DNNNN), (DNND), (NDDN), (NNDD), (DDD)   13

7. (DDDN), (DDND), (DNDD), (NDDD), (DDNNN), (DNDNN), (DNNDN),
   (DNNND), (NDNND), (NNDND), (NNNDD), (NNDDN), (NDNDN), (NDDNN),
   (NNNNNNN), (NNNNND), (NNNNDN), (NNNDNN), (NNDNNN), (NDNNNN),
   (DNNNNN)   21

8. 34

Tallying Tokens

Game tokens from a token machine cost 5 cents each. The machine can handle nickels (N) or dimes (D) only. The machine's programming is sensitive to the order the coins are inserted. Inserting a nickel followed by a dime is a different way to pay than inserting a dime followed by a nickel, even though the amount of money is the same.

Find out how many different ways you can pay for one game token, two tokens, and so on. Complete the following chart.

Number of Tokens	Ways to Pay	Number of Ways
1	(*N*)	1
2	(*NN*) (*D*)	2
3	(*NNN*) (*ND*) (*DN*)	3
4		
5		
6		
7		

How many different ways does the machine need to be programmed to accept payment for 8 tokens?

List as many ways as you can find.

TO THE TEACHER

Branches Going Bonkers

CONNECTIONS	botany • problem solving • patterns
MATERIALS	copy of Activity 7
GROUPING	1 to 3
DURATION	15 minutes
NOTES	Some plants, including algae and root systems, really do branch this way, though there are other identifiable methods of branching. Botanists suggest a chemical inhibitor keeps one branch resting so all the energy of the plant can be directed into the other branch.
ALERT!	After a branch has rested, it is ready to branch again and the process repeats itself. Students sometimes get so caught up in the branching, they lose the ones that have rested.
EXTENSION	Look for other Fibonacci numbers lurking elsewhere in the final branched plant.
MORE INFORMATION	*Fascinating Fibonaccis,* chapter 2, pages 12–13
ANSWERS	**1.** 89 **2.** 15th week

NAME _____

Branches Going Bonkers

Growing plants branch in a variety of different ways. One way follows this rule:

1. The plant branches into two parts.

2. At the next opportunity to branch, only one part branches. The other rests from branching, but still grows.

3. The rested part is ready to branch into two parts at the following opportunity.

4. This pattern continues indefinitely.

The opportunities to branch occur at regular intervals. In this problem, those intervals are weeks.

	Number of Branches
Week 7	
Week 6	
Week 5	
Week 4	
Week 3	← 3
Week 2	← 2

branches · rests · ready to branch

branches · rests

Plant

Sketch the branching of this plant. Examine the number of branches at each interval.

1. Viewed horizontally, how many branches would you expect to find the 10th week?_____

2. Though the branches would be difficult to count, when would you expect there to be about 1,000 branches?_____

Raising Rabbits

CONNECTIONS   math history • problem solving • patterns

MATERIALS   copy of Activity 8

GROUPING   2 to 4

DURATION   20 minutes

NOTES   It is this problem in Fibonacci's book *Liber Abaci* that established the Fibonacci sequence of numbers around A.D. 1200. It is famous in mathematical literature. Though Isaac Asimov referred to it as "that confusing rabbit problem," efforts have been made here to make it understandable. This is, of course, a hypothetical problem—rabbits do not breed like this.

To get started, it helps to designate an adult pair *A*. The first adult pair is in the pen. At the start of every month, add a new *B* (for baby) for every *A* in the pen. All old *B*s become *A*s. Cross out the old *B*s and change them to *A*s, but do not add babies for them yet. They simply mature that month and wait until the next month to start having their own babies. Keeping old *B*s separate from new *B*s can be a problem. It might help to generate the new *B*s first (one for every *A*) and then go back to the old *B*s, scratch them out and make them *A*s. It won't take too much of this before the pattern becomes apparent.

ALERT!   This entire problem is about *pairs* of rabbits.

Once an adult pair is established in the pen, it is there forever! There are no deaths in this problem. Each pair gives birth to a new baby pair every month forever.

EXTENSIONS   • Find out how many pairs of rabbits are in the pen after 5 years and after 10 years.

• Find out when there will be 1 billion rabbits.

MORE INFORMATION   *Fascinating Fibonaccis,* chapter 1; chapter 5, pages 41–43

The Golden Section, chapter 8, pages 61–63

ANSWERS   The column of baby pairs has 0 in January, 1 in February, and 1 in March, and extends through the Fibonacci sequence until there are 89 in December.

The column of adult pairs has 1 in January and 1 in February, and extends through the Fibonacci sequence until there are 144 in December.

The column of total pairs has 1 in January and 2 in February, and extends through the Fibonacci sequence until there are 233 in December.

1. The Fibonacci sequence   **2.** 8,362 rabbits, or 4,181 pairs

3. April of yet the next year—when there are 500,000 pairs

ACTIVITY

8

NAME _____

Raising Rabbits

Begin with one adult pair of rabbits in a pen in January.

Let them multiply according to these rules.

1. Each month, all *Adult* pairs have a *Baby* pair.

2. All old *Baby* pairs simply become *Adults* after a month. *(Baby pairs do not have babies until after they become adult pairs!)*

Complete this chart showing the number of rabbits in the pen each month. Assume none die.

	Baby pairs	Adult pairs	Total pairs
Jan.	0	1	1
Feb.	1	1	2
Mar.			
Apr.			
May			
June			
July			
Aug.			
Sept.			
Oct.			
Nov.			
Dec.			

1. What pattern can you identify here?

2. How many rabbits would you expect to find in June of the following year?_____

3. When will there be 1 million rabbits in the pen?_____

TO THE TEACHER

Pleasure Plotting

CONNECTIONS	coordinate graphing • math history
MATERIALS	copy of Activity 9 • straightedge • copy of coordinate graph paper page 30 copy of Supplement 2 and copy of coordinate graph paper page 31 (for Extensions)
GROUPING	individuals
DURATION	30 minutes
NOTES	Have students do this activity individually with their own straightedges and coordinate graph (page 30). You may want to make a transparency of page 29. This likeness of Fibonacci is taken from *Fascinating Fibonaccis.* A traditional likeness of him is part of a collection of famous mathematicians housed at Columbia University. There is also a statue of him in the Scott Garden in Pisa, Italy. It bears little resemblance to the other two likenesses. Other than the likelihood that he wore medieval garments, little is known about Fibonacci's appearance.
ALERT!	You may need to remind even experienced plotters that the first coordinate is the horizontal one and the second is vertical. All the fractions here are $\frac{1}{2}$.
EXTENSIONS	• Use supplement 2 (page 67) and the grid on page 31 to create the same picture using all four quadrants and negative coordinates. • Using a likeness of Fibonacci you find in a math textbooks, design a similar activity using different coordinates. • Use a graphing calculator to draw this graph.
MORE INFORMATION	*Fascinating Fibonaccis,* chapter 8
ANSWERS	

Activity 9

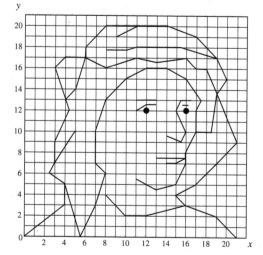

Supplement 2

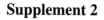
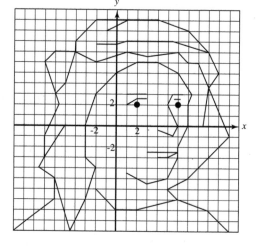

NAME _____

Pleasure Plotting

On a coordinate grid, plot the following points according to the numbered directions.

End means lift your pencil and begin again with the next numbered direction.

Reminder! (4, 3) means 4 across, plot first, 3 up, plot last.

1. Connect (0, 0) to (4, 3) (4, 5). End.
2. Connect (8, 4) to (10, 2) to (12, 2) to (16, 3). End.
3. Connect (11, 13) to (13, 13). End.
4. Connect (11, 12) to (12, $12\frac{1}{2}$) to (13, $12\frac{1}{2}$). End.
5. Connect (14, $9\frac{1}{2}$) to ($15\frac{1}{2}$, 9) to (16, 10) to (15, 12) to ($15\frac{1}{2}$, 13) to ($16\frac{1}{2}$, 13). End.
7. Connect ($15\frac{1}{2}$, $12\frac{1}{2}$) to ($16\frac{1}{2}$, $12\frac{1}{2}$). End.
8. Connect (13, $7\frac{1}{2}$) to (16, $7\frac{1}{2}$) to (15, 7) to (14, 7). End.
9. Connect the columns of points in order top to bottom. Begin with the column to the left.

(11, $5\frac{1}{2}$)	(5, 14)	(5, 10)	(21, 0)	(11, 20)
(13, $4\frac{1}{2}$)	(4, 13)	(3, 7)	(19, 2)	(8, 20)
(15, 5)	($4\frac{1}{2}$, 12)	($2\frac{1}{2}$, 6)	(16, 3)	(6, 18)
(16, 7)	(3, 9)	(4, 5)	(15, 4)	(6, 17)
(16, 8)	(3, 7)	($5\frac{1}{2}$, 0)	(17, 5)	(4, 17)
(17, 10)	End	(7, 3)	(21, 9)	(3, 16)
($18\frac{1}{2}$, 10)		(8, 6)	(19, $13\frac{1}{2}$)	(4, 13)
(19, $13\frac{1}{2}$)		(7, 7)	(20, 15)	End
(18, 16)		(7, 10)	(19, 17)	(8, $17\frac{1}{2}$)
(17, 16)		(8, 13)	(17, 19)	(10, $17\frac{1}{2}$)
(16, 17)		(10, 15)	(14, 20)	(11, 18)
(13, $16\frac{1}{2}$)		(12, 16)	(11, 20)	(15, 18)
(11, 17)		(14, 16)	(9, 19)	(19, 17)
(8, 16)		(16, 15)	End	End
(6, 17)		($17\frac{1}{2}$, 13)		
		(17, 12)		
		(17, 10)		
		End		

10. Center two small circles at (12, 12) and (16, 12). Fill in these circles (mostly, but leave a twinkle!).

NAME _____

Pleasure Plotting

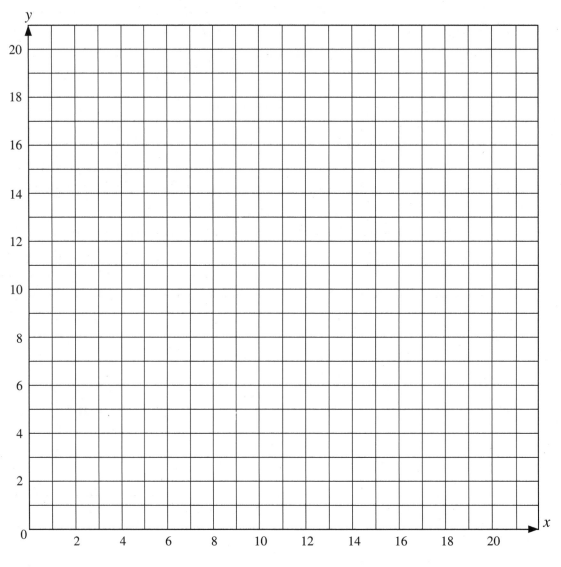

Fibonacci

NAME _____

Pleasure Plotting

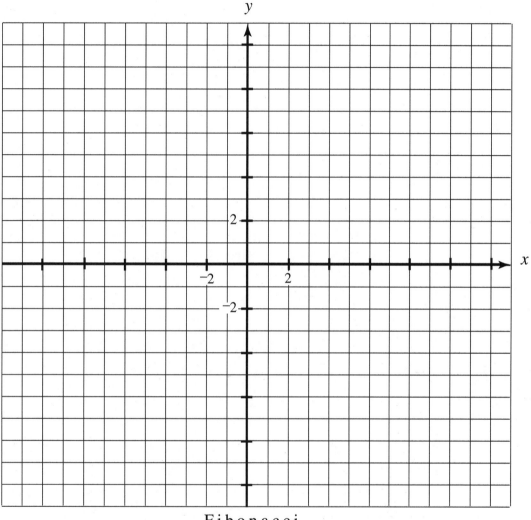

Fibonacci

Prickly Pinecones

CONNECTIONS | life science • nature • patterns

MATERIALS | collection of pinecones • felt markers in two dark colors
copy of Activity 10 • good example of pinecone with rows of bracts
already marked

GROUPING | 2

DURATION | 20–50 minutes

NOTES | Ideally, each student gets one pinecone, although one per pair or trio would be adequate. Before the activity, ask students to bring in pinecones. Give each student a copy of the activity and two markers that are dark enough to show up on the pinecone. Have students work in pairs, so they can share their colored cones. This activity could take up to 50 minutes if you have many pinecones and curious students.

Make sure students understand how to find Fibonacci numbers in the rows of pinecones. Once they learn this, they can easily find Fibonacci numbers in artichokes, pineapples, sunflowers, and elsewhere using a similar technique.

ALERT! | Be sure the pine cones are dry, in good shape, and relatively young. The more pinecones you can assemble from different trees the better. Closed cones generally work better than open ones, but not necessarily; some open ones are easy to count, and closed ones sometimes carry too much sticky pitch. Smashed or half-eaten pinecones do not work!

A common error is to count the number of bracts in a row. What is being counted is the number of similar rows.

EXTENSIONS | • Gather wet pinecones and study their configurations. See if they change to a different Fibonacci number when they dry.

• Look for pinecones with a third row of bracts. This can be the case if the bracts are somewhat hexagonal in shape. Is there also a Fibonacci number of rows of that third row?

• Of the two different rows of bracts on a typical pinecone, one will always be steeper than the other, which is more shallow. Investigate whether the steep or shallow row is the higher Fibonacci number.

MORE INFORMATION | *Fascinating Fibonaccis,* chapter 2, pages 6–9

ANSWERS | **1–5**.   All pairs should be adjacent Fibonacci numbers. 2, 3 or 3, 5 or 5, 8 or 8, 13. The written conclusion should reflect this.

Extension: The steep row is a higher Fibonacci number. An interesting discussion might focus on the geometrical reasons for this.

10 Prickly Pinecones

1. Hold a pinecone carefully in your hands. Identify a row of bracts, the petals of pinecones. Bracts fall into rows that continue up and around the cone. Color the entire length of that one row with a felt marker, as shown in the picture.

   How many rows of bracts on your pinecone go the same way as the one you colored? Use the colored one as your first row and count similar rows "parallel" to it. Stop counting when you reach the colored row again.

2. Find another row of bracts that crosses the one you already colored because it goes in the opposite direction. Color that one row with a marker—a different color, if possible.

   How many rows of bracts on your pinecone are similar to and parallel to the new one you just colored? Remember to count the colored one.

3. Repeat this procedure with a different pinecone. Trade pinecones with a classmate (or another group) or find a new one. Select one that
   • is a different size

   • has more or fewer bracts

   • looks different

   How many rows of bracts did you find like the first colored row? _____

   How many rows of bracts did you find like the second colored row? _____

4. Repeat the steps using other pinecones.

   Record the numbers of rows going two ways. _____ _____

5. What conclusions can you draw about the numbers of similar rows of bracts on pinecones?

TO THE TEACHER

Rational (and Decimal) Ratios

CONNECTIONS	calculator studies • patterns
MATERIALS	copy of Activity 11 • calculator
GROUPING	2 to 4
DURATION	20 minutes
NOTES	This straightforward exercise shows how ratios of Fibonacci numbers converge (draw close) to the golden ratio. As Activity 14 points out, the ratio of adjacent terms in any Fibonacci-like sequence will converge to the golden ratio, but the Fibonacci numbers are the simplest of these and converge the quickest.
	Consider doing Activity 14 as a follow-up activity.
ALERT!	Students need to round accurately.
EXTENSION	Design a computer program to generate the golden ratio using Fibonacci numbers.
MORE INFORMATION	*Fascinating Fibonaccis,* chapter 3, page 23

ANSWERS				
5	$\dfrac{5}{8}$	0.625000	$\dfrac{5}{3}$	1.666667
8	$\dfrac{8}{13}$	0.615385	$\dfrac{8}{5}$	1.600000
13	$\dfrac{13}{21}$	0.619048	$\dfrac{13}{8}$	1.625000
21	$\dfrac{21}{34}$	0.617647	$\dfrac{21}{13}$	1.615385
34	$\dfrac{34}{55}$	0.618182	$\dfrac{34}{21}$	1.619048
55	$\dfrac{55}{89}$	0.617978	$\dfrac{55}{34}$	1.617647
89	$\dfrac{89}{144}$	0.618056	$\dfrac{89}{55}$	1.618182
144	$\dfrac{144}{233}$	0.618026	$\dfrac{144}{89}$	1.617978
233	$\dfrac{233}{377}$	0.618037	$\dfrac{233}{144}$	1.618056
377	$\dfrac{377}{601}$	0.618032	$\dfrac{377}{233}$	1.618026

Conclusion: The larger the two consecutive Fibonacci numbers, the closer the ratio of the two numbers will be to the golden ratio, 0.618. . . or 1.618. . . .

Rational (and Decimal) Ratios

The Fibonacci sequence is 1, 1, 2, 3, 5, 8, and so on. Each number is the sum of the previous two numbers. List the Fibonacci numbers in the left column, then complete the table. Round to six decimal places.

Fibonacci Numbers	Ratio: $\dfrac{\text{Fibonacci number}}{\text{next larger F number}}$ = Decimal		Ratio: $\dfrac{\text{Fibonacci number}}{\text{next smaller F number}}$ = Decimal	
1	$\dfrac{1}{1}$	1.000000	$\varnothing$	$\varnothing$
1	$\dfrac{1}{2}$	0.500000	$\dfrac{2}{1}$	1.000000
2	$\dfrac{2}{3}$	0.666667	$\dfrac{2}{1}$	2.000000
3	$\dfrac{3}{5}$	0.600000	$\dfrac{3}{2}$	1.500000
5	$\dfrac{5}{8}$	____	$\dfrac{5}{3}$	____
8	____	____	____	____
____	____	____	____	____
____	____	____	____	____
____	____	____	____	____
____	____	____	____	____
____	____	____	____	____
____	____	____	____	____
____	____	____	____	____

Examine the decimal equivalents of the Fibonacci ratios in this table. What comments or conclusions might you make?

Beautiful Problems

CONNECTIONS	proportion • art
MATERIALS	copy of Activity 12
GROUPING	1 or 2
DURATION	10 minutes
NOTES	Fibonacci numbers provide an easy way to approximate the golden ratio. But this is only useful when one of the dimensions is (or can be) a Fibonacci number of units.

When this is not the case, students can multiply the smaller dimension (usually the width) by 1.618 to find the larger dimension, or multiply the larger by 0.618 to find the smaller dimension.

Students can use proportions to solve for the missing dimension.

$$\frac{\text{small}}{\text{large}} = \frac{0.6181}{1}$$

The questions point out how pervasive the golden rectangle is in our daily lives (paperback novels, light-switch plates, and so on). Many examples, such as credit cards and hand-held calculators, are believed to be related to the dimensions of the hand.

ALERT!	It is important to distinguish the small and large dimensions when solving these problems. Often, small is the width and large is the length.
EXTENSION	Search for other golden rectangles existing in the world around you.
MORE INFORMATION	*Fascinating Fibonaccis,* chapter 3
	The Golden Section, chapter 7
ANSWERS	1. 34 in., 55 cm
	2. no, yes, no
	3. 27.8 cm
	4. 5 in.
	5. 17 cm
	6. 7.1 cm
	7. 4 ft
	8. 8.9 ft

NAME _____

Beautiful Problems

Certain rectangles are especially pleasing to the eye. They are not too wide and not too long. They are called golden rectangles.

The proportions of such rectangles are shown here.

Rectangles whose side measurements are consecutive Fibonacci numbers larger than 5 are also golden—the numbers provide an easy way to achieve the golden ratio. The Fibonacci numbers are 1, 1, 2, 3, 5, 8, and so on, where each number is the sum of the previous two numbers.

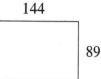

Keep this in mind as you answer these questions.

1. An artist wishes to paint in the shape of the golden rectangle. If the paper is 21 inches wide, how long should it be? _____

   If it is 89 centimeters long, how wide should it be? _____

2. A standard piece of computer paper is $8\frac{1}{2}$ inches wide and 11 inches long. Is it a golden rectangle? _____ too wide? _____ too long? _____

3. A sketch of the front view of the Parthenon, which has golden proportions, is 45 centimeters long. How high should it be?

   Hint: $\dfrac{\text{large}}{\text{small}} = \dfrac{0.618}{1}$

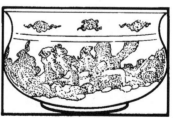

4. A bowl dating to the Ching dynasty in China has an 8-inch diameter at the top. How deep is it if it exhibits golden proportions? _____

5. A standard paperback novel is a golden rectangle 10.5 centimeters wide. How high is a standard paperback? _____

6. A standard, single light-switch plate is 11.5 centimeters long. If it is a golden rectangle, how wide is it? _____

7. A carpenter wishes to install some doors to a patio that are visually pleasing. If the doors need to be $6\frac{1}{2}$ feet high, how wide should they be? _____

8. A Navajo rug being woven is 5.5 feet wide. To have golden proportions, the person weaving it should stop after how many feet of length? _____

Pieces of Gold

CONNECTIONS	geometry • constructions
MATERIALS	copy of Activity 13 • compass
GROUPING	1 to 3
DURATION	15 minutes
NOTES	Give each student a copy of the activity.

Students can easily recognize real-world golden rectangles by this characteristic: All are dividable into a square and a new rectangle of the same proportions as the original. This investigation drives home that point.

In theory, this division into a square and a new rectangle can go on forever. In fact, however, human error and pencil thickness make that impossible.

Any golden rectangle can be separated into a square and another golden rectangle. In this activity, however, the squares have successive Fibonacci number dimensions. This points out the relationship between the numbers and the proportion.

ALERT!   Students may become frustrated if they do not understand how to do the spiral. Students need to swing quarter-circle arcs through each square a quarter circle at a time, then reposition the compass at the appropriate corner of the next smaller square before drawing a new quarter circle. The diagram helps by showing dark points at the corners where students need to place the compass point.

EXTENSION   Using a new piece of graph paper, do the drawing in reverse. Begin in the center of the paper by outlining a square the size of one of the small boxes of the graph paper. Then outline another box next to it. Attach to these two boxes a square 2 units on a side so one large square touches both boxes. Identify a 3-unit edge onto which attach a square 3 units on a side. Identify a 5-unit edge and attach a square 5 units on a side. Then repeat for an 8-unit edge. Attach these squares in a systematic spiral formation. Use a compass and swing quarter-circle arcs to unify these squares with a spiral.

MORE INFORMATION   *Fascinating Fibonaccis,* chapter 2, pages 14–15, and chapter 3, page 22

The Golden Section, chapter 7

ANSWERS   Students' results should look like the diagram.

Pieces of Gold

Pictured below is a graph-paper golden rectangle. It is golden because its width and length are consecutive Fibonacci numbers of units that approximate the golden ratio 0.618. Fibonacci numbers are 1, 1, 2, 3, 5, 8, and so on where each number is the sum of the previous two numbers.

This investigation will help you understand the special characteristics of this rectangle.

1. Draw a vertical line dividing the rectangle into a square on the left and another rectangle to the right of the square.

2. Look at the new rectangle, which is also golden. Draw a line separating it into a square on the top and another rectangle below the square.

3. Look at this new rectangle, also golden. Separate it into a square on the right and a rectangle to the left of the square.

4. Separate the new golden rectangle into a square on the bottom and a golden rectangle above the square.

5. Separate the new golden rectangle into a square on the left and a golden rectangle to the right of the square.

6. Using this diagram as your guide, can you construct a golden spiral in the golden rectangle using a compass? Begin by drawing a quarter-circle arc in the largest square as shown in the diagram. Then draw an arc in the second largest square the same way. Continue until the arcs are too small to draw.

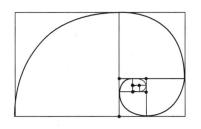

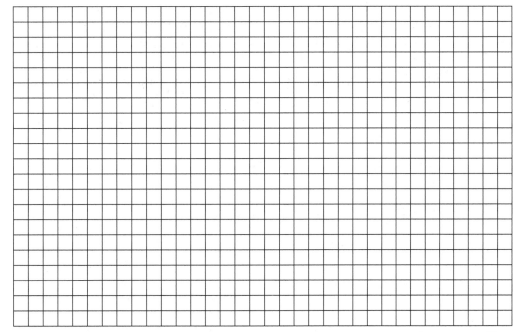

Invent Your Own Numbers

CONNECTIONS	calculator studies • patterns
MATERIALS	copy of Activity 14 • calculator
GROUPING	1 or 2
DURATION	15 minutes
NOTES	Give each student a copy of the activity.

This activity's important point is that any Fibonacci-type sequence will produce ratios of adjacent numbers that get closer and closer to the golden ratio. The Fibonacci sequence is the most simple of these. It includes the smallest integers that produce the ratio.

ALERT! Students may not realize they can start with any number—positive, negative, fractional, huge, tiny, or a combination of these! When they do realize this, their numbers will probably get wacky—hence the instruction to memorize them is given somewhat in jest!

EXTENSION Investigate different sequences of numbers to determine what affects the speed with which the ratios of adjacent numbers reach 0.618.

MORE INFORMATION *Fascinating Fibonaccis,* chapter 3, pages 23

ANSWERS The numbers and the ratios will differ for each student. However, the ratios should clearly get closer and closer to 0.618.

14 Invent Your Own Numbers

Is your last name Washington? Wong? Smith? Sanchez? Why not invent your very own Fibonacci-type sequence of numbers and give it your very own name?

The Fibonacci sequence is 1, 1, 2, 3, 5, 8, and so on where each number is the sum of the previous two numbers.

Numbers	Ratios

1. Begin with any number.

2. Decide on any second number.

3. Each number from now on is the sum of the two numbers preceding it. Determine the next 12 numbers in your sequence.

Kapoor-Lee
Numbers

4. Name your numbers your last name, or anything you wish! _____

5. Memorize your numbers. After all, they are your very own numbers!

6. Determine the ratio of each of your numbers divided by the next larger number in your sequence (rounded to three decimal places). Write each ratio on the line next to each number.

7. Write your conclusions about the ratio of consecutive numbers in your sequence, especially as the numbers get larger.

Tantalizing Triangles

CONNECTIONS	geometry • visual thinking
MATERIALS	copy of Activity 15 • colored pencils • copy of Supplement 3
GROUPING	2 to 4
DURATION	20 minutes
NOTES	Give each student a copy of this activity. The colored pencils will help them identify triangles. Sensitizing students to these triangle shapes, as with the golden rectangle shapes, will help them identify these shapes outside the classroom.
ALERT!	Students must organize their methods of counting triangles. They should first identify the various sizes, then count them. Or they could count all the solid-line triangles, all the dotted-line triangles, and then anything that wasn't yet counted. Students may use the additional pentagons on page 68 to sort out the triangles.
EXTENSION	If there were yet another pentagram (a star within a pentagon) inside the dotted pentagon, how many of each kind of triangle would there be?
MORE INFORMATION	*Fascinating Fibonaccis,* chapter 7, pages 82–83
ANSWERS	

1. 20

5 light-gray size
5 dark-gray size
10 striped size

2. 15

5 light-gray size
5 dark-gray size
5 striped size

3. 85 (double the answers to 1 and 2 plus those triangles pictured here, 5 light-gray size and 10 dark-gray size)

    40 shape A
    45 shape B

Extension: $135 = (3 \times 35) + 15 + 15$

NAME _____

Tantalizing Triangles

Two kinds of triangles have golden proportions. In both cases, the ratio of the short side to the long side is the same—the golden ratio, 0.618. . . to 1.

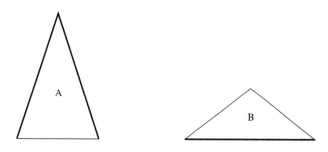

Shape *A* has two long sides and one short side.

Shape *B* has two short sides and one long side.

1. In the large, solid-lined figure, how many shape *A* golden triangles are there of any size? _____

2. In the large, solid-lined figure, how many shape *B* golden triangles are there of any size? _____

3. Including the dotted-lined figure, how many golden triangles of either shape and of any size can you find? _____

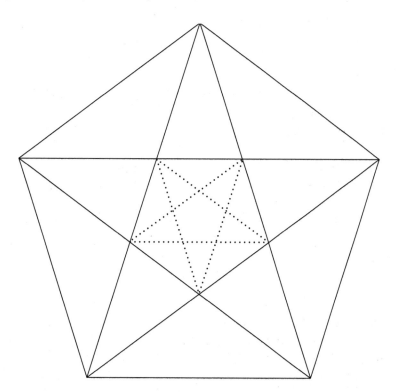

TO THE TEACHER

Pentagon Play

CONNECTIONS	geometry • visual thinking
MATERIALS	copy of Activity 16 • scissors
GROUPING	2 to 4
DURATION	20 minutes
NOTES	Give each student a copy of the activity. This activity provides a hands-on experience with pentagons and golden triangles. Both figures are fascinating mathematically and in their relationship to each other.
ALERT!	Getting the large pentagon from the 12 pieces is a sophisticated task that slower or younger students might find frustrating. However, many students will enjoy the challenge.
	Students should fold the strip of paper into a knot very gently. If they do not tear the paper, a true pentagon emerges.
EXTENSION	If a star is inscribed in a regular pentagon, you will find no fewer than 25 occurrences of the golden ratio. Investigate this by drawing a star in a regular pentagon (making it a pentagram), lettering all vertices, and writing down all the ratios that qualify.
MORE INFORMATION	*Fascinating Fibonaccis,* chapter 2, pages 17–18; chapter 3, pages 20–21
	The Golden Section, chapters 5 and 6
ANSWERS	**1.** 5 **2.** 2 **3.** 4 **4.** 2

5.

```
        5    4
   11  12      10
     1        2

   6    3    9
    7        8
```

6. Only one golden triangle is visible on the surface of the folded pentagon, but if the figure is held up to the light, many others emerge.

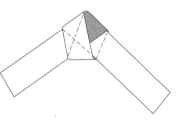

NAME _____

Pentagon Play

Cut out the five pentagons at the bottom of the sheet. Cut two of them into the additional pieces as marked. You will then have three pentagons and nine golden isosceles triangles. They are golden because the ratio of the short sides to the long sides is 0.618 to 1. They are isosceles because two sides are the same.

1. How many of the triangles have two short sides and one long side? _____

2. How many different sizes are there of these short-sided triangles? _____

3. How many of the triangles have two long sides and one short side? _____

4. How many different sizes are there of these long-sided triangles? _____

5. Fit all 12 pieces together into one large pentagon.

6. Cut a strip of paper 1 in. wide and about 11 in. long. Fold it into a flat knot—very gently! Can you get a perfect pentagon? Find the golden triangles in your folded paper.

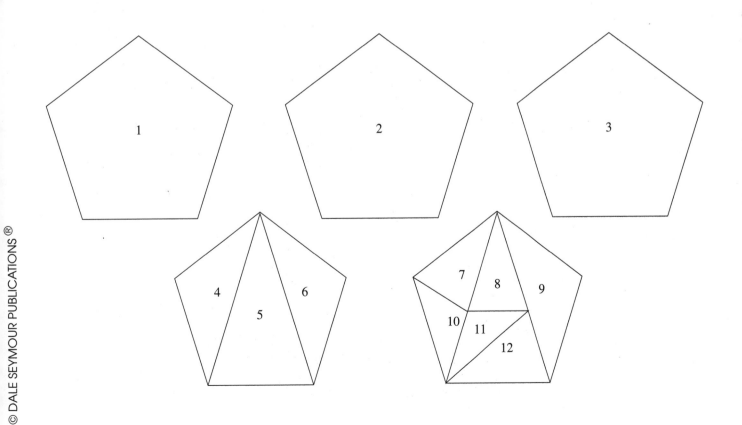

Fibonacci Mystery

CONNECTIONS	geometry • visual thinking • algebra
MATERIALS	copy of Activity 17 • straightedge or ruler copy of Supplement 4 (for Extension)
GROUPING	1 or 2
DURATION	15 minutes
NOTES	This is a classic problem, and a classic case of brainwashing! Set out as convincingly as this, few students will consider the possibility that the pieces of square really do not fit into the rectangle.
	Algebra students can explore and compare the slope of the line that divides *C* and *D* and the slope of the diagonal that divides A and B. The slopes are not equal, so the two lines cannot each be part of the diagonal of the rectangle, which would make them collinear.
ALERT!	Students may have difficulty sectioning the grids in questions 6 and 7. Point out that the dimensions of the sections must also be Fibonacci numbers. The 13-unit sides are divided into 5 and 8 units; the 8-unit sides are divided into 5 and 3 units.
EXTENSION	Despite how it appears, the rectangles do not fit. One piece is missing. Using the additional grids on page 69, section other Fibonacci squares. Cut out the pieces to the find the missing piece.
MORE INFORMATION	*Fascinating Fibonaccis,* chapter 7, pages 84 and 89
	The Golden Section, chapter 9, pages 75–80
ANSWERS	**1.** 64 **2.** 65 **3.** Areas are different. **4.** 25
	5. 24 **6.** 169 **7.** 168

8. The edges that make up what appears to be the diagonal of the rectangle are not, in fact, collinear. They do not line up and the gap (or overlap) that exists adds up to a little 1-unit space.

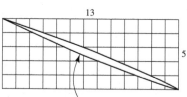

space or overlap

NAME _____

Fibonacci Mystery

Consider a square 8 units on a side cut into sections A, B, C, and D, then rearranged into a new rectangle.

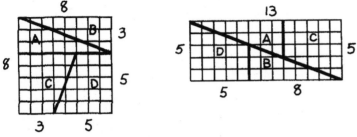

1. What is the area of the original square? _____

2. What is the area of the new rectangle? _____

3. What is odd here? _____

What you discovered in questions 1 and 2 happens with any Fibonacci square, a square whose side is a Fibonacci number that is divided into sections whose length and width are smaller Fibonacci numbers. Fibonacci numbers are 1, 1, 2, 3, 5, 8, and so on where each number is the sum of the previous two numbers. For example, look at this square:

Square   **Sections**   **Rectangle**

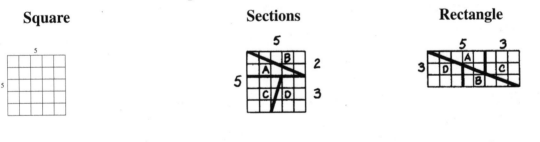

4. What is the area of the square? _____   5. What is the area of rectangle? _____

Sketch in the sections for this square and rectangle. Remember, the dimensions of your sections must also be Fibonacci numbers.

Square   **Rectangle**

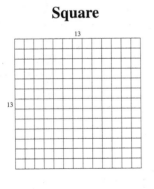

6. What is the area of square? _____   7. What is the area of rectangle? _____

8. What is your explanation? _____

TO THE TEACHER

Fibonacci Tree

CONNECTIONS	binary numbers
MATERIALS	copy of Activity 18
GROUPING	1 to 3
DURATION	30–40 minutes
NOTES	Give each student a copy of the activity.

The importance of binary numerals today is their use in computers. Since there are two symbols, a switch or light can be on or off. The light is on or off, or the current can pass through or cannot pass through.

ALERT!

You may need to give students more direction regarding writing binary numerals. These practice numerals might help. They could be done together before getting started on the activity.

In binary numerals, each place value (moving to the left) is two times the previous place value. The first eight place values are 128, 64, 32, 16, 8, 4, 2, and 1.

Decimal	Binary	Decimal	Binary
10	1010 (8 + 2)	57	111001
25	11001	82	1010010
40	101000 (32 + 8)	117	1110101 (64 + 32 + 16 + 4 + 1)

EXTENSIONS

ANSWER

- Make a holiday tree. Use red and green as the colors and place a star on the top of the tree!

- Do the activity on a bigger piece of graph paper all the way up to 50 Fibonacci numbers.

- Use other number bases requiring 3, 4, 5, or more symbols or colors. For example, tertiary (base 3) numerals require three symbols; each place value is three times the previous one.

- Use *Lucas numbers,* numbers generated like Fibonacci numbers, but the sequence begins with 1 and 3, rather than 1 and 1.

NAME _____

Fibonacci Tree

Binary numerals are constructed in the same manner as decimal numerals, with two important exceptions:

- Each successive place value is two times rather than ten times the previous value.

- There are only two symbols (0, 1) rather than ten (0, 1, 2, 3, 4, 5, 6, 7, 8, 9).

Decimal	8s	4s	2s	1s	Binary
1				1	1
2			1	0	10
3			1	1	11
4		1	0	0	100
5		1	0	1	101

For example: The number thirteen can be written both as a decimal numeral and as a binary numeral:

         10 1   (place values)
Decimal   1 3   because $(1 \times 10) + (3 \times 1)$ is thirteen

         8 4 2 1 (place values)
Binary   1 1 0 1 because $(1 \times 8) + (1 \times 4) + (0 \times 2) + (1 \times 1)$ is thirteen

Express the first 25 Fibonacci numbers as binary numerals. Fibonacci numbers are 1, 1, 2, 3, 5, 8, and so on where each number is the sum of the previous two numbers. Using a solid square to represent 1 and an open square to represent 0 (or different colors or shades of green for the two symbols), record the numerals on the left half of this tree. The numerals will become larger as you move down the tree. On the right side of the trunk, show the reflection of the left side. The first six numerals have been done for you.

TO THE TEACHER

Hairy Calculating

CONNECTIONS	calculator studies • order of operations
MATERIALS	copy of Activity 19 • calculator
GROUPING	1 to 4
DURATION	20 minutes
NOTES	To use the formula, students need calculators that can raise to powers and take square roots.

J. P. M. Binet derived this formula for finding the *n*th Fibonacci number before the numbers were named *Fibonacci* by Edouard Lucas. It is usually expressed this way:

$$\frac{1}{\sqrt{5}}\left(\frac{1+\sqrt{5}}{2}\right)^n - \frac{1}{\sqrt{5}}\left(\frac{1-\sqrt{5}}{2}\right)^n$$

ALERT!

Students must observe the grouping symbols (fraction lines and parentheses). The exact calculator routine will vary from one calculator to another, but the *equals* key or *enter* key will group whenever grouping is indicated.

EXTENSION

Investigate the significance of the second term when *n* gets very large. At what *n* can you determine the number from your calculator without using the second term?

MORE INFORMATION

Fascinating Fibonaccis, chapter 8, page 95

ANSWERS

1. 10,946

2. 5,702,887

3. 5.7314784×10^{20}

NAME _____

Hairy Calculating

The Fibonacci sequence is 1, 1, 2, 3, 5, 8, and so on where each number is the sum of the two previous numbers. There is a formula for determining the *n*th Fibonacci number; *n* can represent any number. Using this formula, you can determine any counting number in the Fibonacci sequence! For example, you can determine the fifth Fibonacci number by substituting 5 for *n* in the formula. You can determine the thirteenth Fibonacci number by substituting 13 for *n*.

The *n*th Fibonacci number = 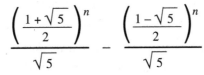 $\dfrac{\left(\dfrac{1+\sqrt{5}}{2}\right)^n}{\sqrt{5}} - \dfrac{\left(\dfrac{1-\sqrt{5}}{2}\right)^n}{\sqrt{5}}$

Binet's Formula

Be very careful using this formula with your calculator. Observe the grouping symbols (fraction lines, parentheses) by using the equals key to group appropriately.

Consider calculating the second half of the formula first and entering it into the memory. Then calculate the first half and subtract the second half by calling it up from the memory.

- Since the third Fibonacci number is 2, test the formula by using 3 for *n* and see if you get 2.

- Since the fifth Fibonacci number is 5, test the formula by using 5 for *n* and see if you get 5.

After you are comfortable using the formula and you know you are using it correctly, determine the following:

1. 21st Fibonacci number

2. 34th Fibonacci number

3. 101st Fibonacci number in scientific notation (for example, 1996 in scientific notation is 1.996×10^3)

TO THE TEACHER

Fibonacci's Favorites
Part I

CONNECTIONS	algebra • problem solving • math history
MATERIALS	copy of Activity 20
GROUPING	1 to 3
DURATION	20 minutes
NOTES	Give each student a copy of this activity. *Liber Abaci* has many problems similar to those so popular in the problem-solving arena today.
ALERT!	These sophisticated problems are best suited to students who have some knowledge of algebra. The first problem can be done without algebra, but could benefit from that kind of reasoning.
MORE INFORMATION	*Fascinating Fibonaccis,* chapter 1, page 1, and chapter 8

ANSWERS

1. No. The man with three loaves should have taken 4 bezants leaving 1 for the other man. In addition to the bezants they received, the two men ate equally. So what they received totally was not in the 2 to 3 ratio, it was in a 1 to 4 ratio.

    Each participant in the meal ate $\frac{5}{3}$ loaves. One man only brought $\frac{6}{3}$ loaves, so only contributed $\frac{1}{3}$ loaf to the soldier. The other man brought $\frac{9}{3}$ loaves so contributed $\frac{4}{3}$ loaf to the soldier. Their respective contributions to the soldier were in ratio 1 to 4.

2. The first has 15 denarii, the second has 3 denarii, the third has 9 denarii, and the fourth has 19 denarii. This problem is best done using a system of equations: If first = a, second = b, third = c, and fourth = d; then, $a + b + c = 27$, $b + c + d = 31$, $c + d + a = 43$, and $d + a + b = 37$.

ACTIVITY

20

NAME _____

Fibonacci Favorites
Part I

These problems were taken from a famous math book, *Liber Abaci*, written by the mathematician Fibonacci around the beginning of the thirteenth century.

1. There were two men, of whom the first had 3 small loaves of bread and the other 2; they walked to a spring where they sat down and ate. A soldier joined them and shared their meal, each of the three men eating the same amount. When all the bread was eaten, the soldier departed, leaving 5 bezants to pay for his meal. The first man accepted 3 of the bezants, since he had had 3 loaves; the other took the remaining 2 bezants for his two loaves. Was the division fair?

2. There are 4 men of whom the first and the second and the third together have 27 denarii; the second and the third and the fourth together have 31 denarii, the third and the fourth and the first have 43; and the fourth and the first and the second have 37. How much does each have?

TO THE TEACHER
Fibonacci's Favorites Part II

CONNECTIONS	algebra • problem solving • math history
MATERIALS	copy of Activity 21
GROUPING	1 to 3
DURATION	20 minutes
NOTES	Give each student a copy of the activity. *Liber Abaci* has many problems similar to those so popular in the problem-solving arena today.
ALERT!	These sophisticated problems are best suited to students who have some knowledge of algebra. The first problem can be done without algebra, but could benefit from that kind of reasoning.
MORE INFORMATION	*Fascinating Fibonaccis,* chapter 1, page 1, chapter 8
ANSWERS	

1. 10.5 denarii

This problem can be done with a simple algebraic equation:

$2(2(2x - 12) - 12) - 12 = 0$

$x = 10.5$

It can also be solved working backward. In Pisa, his doubled money = 12, which means he arrived in Pisa with 6 denarii. In Florence, his doubled money must have been 18, which means he arrived in Florence with 9. In Lucca, his doubled money must have been 21, which means he started with 10.5 denarii.

2. $\frac{60}{37}$ hr, or $1\frac{23}{37}$ hr, or 1.62 hr.

Algebra best solves this problem. If a lion can eat a sheep in 4 hours, it can eat $\frac{1}{4}$ sheep in 1 hour; the leopard can eat $\frac{1}{5}$ in an hour, and the bear can eat $\frac{1}{6}$ in an hour. Multiply the fraction they can each eat per hour by the number of hours they will work at it (x) and set the sum of those fractions equal to one whole sheep.

$\frac{x}{4} + \frac{x}{5} + \frac{x}{6} = 1$
$x = 1.62$

21 Fibonacci's Favorites Part II

The following problems were taken from a famous math book, *Liber Abaci,* written by the mathematician Fibonacci around the beginning of the thirteenth century.

1. A man doing business in Lucca doubled his money there and then spent 12 denarii. He left and went to Florence where he also doubled his money and spent 12 denarii. Traveling to Pisa, he doubled his money and spent 12 denarii. He was then all out of money. How much did he have in the beginning?

2. A lion could eat a sheep in 4 hours. A leopard could eat one in 5 hours, and a bear could eat one in 6 hours. How many hours would it take for all of them to devour a sheep if it were thrown in among them?

Projects and Supplements

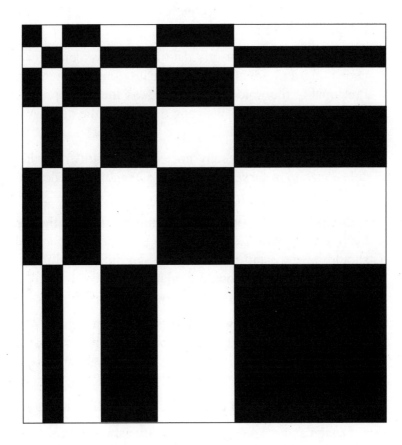

TO THE TEACHER

Rectangle Beauty Contest

CONNECTIONS	proportion • data and statistics • art
MATERIALS	copy of Project 1
GROUPING	individuals
DURATION	30 minutes or more
NOTES	Have students individually gather data and graph it, and then pool their findings in groups or as a class.

Investigations such as this date back many centuries. They are used by the packaging and advertising industries—not to mention school science fairs! Presumably the golden rectangle *D* is the most pleasing to the most people, and rectangles get less pleasing the further the dimensions get from the golden dimensions of 0.618 to 1.

Your students may or may not get this result from their surveys. Many variables operate in surveys, and results cannot be predetermined.

Students may need help with the word *frequency* and with translating the frequencies into a histogram. The numbers used in the frequency column of the histogram will vary depending on the size of the sample. The lowest number should be zero, and the highest no less than the highest frequency found; the horizontal divisions should be determined by dividing that range by the number of divisions desired, and rounding to appropriate numbers.

ALERT! Precede this activity with discussion of data gathering, frequencies, and histograms. This can be an interesting study if students and those they question take it seriously. Instill the value of going about this as a scientific investigation, seeking sincere responses.

EXTENSIONS
- Design and conduct a more elaborate study with more rectangles.

- Design and conduct a similar study asking people to place the crossbar on a cross at the most pleasing place. Then measure where people place the bar, categorize the values, and proceed with an investigation of the most popular placement. What is the ratio of the large segment to the small?

- Use a computer to create your graphics.

MORE INFORMATION *Fascinating Fibonaccis*, chapter 3, page 19–22.

ANSWERS Rectangle D *might* be the most popular because it is a golden rectangle. The answer lies in conducting a scientifically sound investigation, accurately displaying the results, and discussing the results.

PROJECT 1

NAME _____

Rectangle Beauty Contest

Ask your friends, relatives, and neighbors to pick from the set of rectangles the one they consider the most visually pleasing. Ask, "Which is your favorite rectangle?"

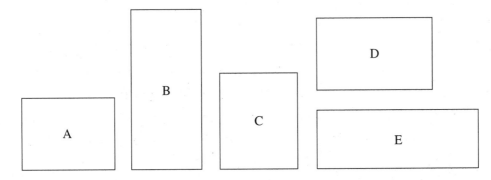

Record your findings, then record the number of tally marks in the frequency column.

Tally (use slashes ⫻⫻⫻ /)	Frequency
A	
B	
C	
D	
E	

Make a graph (also called a histogram) using the data you gathered. On the left, use the numbers for the frequency that will fit your data.

Write a summary of your findings. Include the winning rectangle and its dimensions. Combine your findings with your classmates. What conclusions can you draw?

Favorite Rectangle

Frequency

0

A   B   C   D   E

Rectangle

Rectangle Search

CONNECTIONS   geometry • measurement • statistics • art

MATERIALS   copy of Project 2 • meter stick and ruler • calculator

GROUPING   individuals

DURATION   see Notes

NOTES   The duration of this activity depends on the amount of data students gather. Students may do this activity on their own, or they may collect data at home, complete the work in class, and pool their results.

While many rectangles do not exhibit the golden ratio, the ratios of the dimensions of rectangles in a group may average an approximation to the golden ratio: $0.618 \pm 10\%$, which is 0.56 to 0.68.

ALERT!   Students should measure carefully. Metric measurements work best. Furthermore, students must examine all rectangles in the category; selectivity of any kind would alter the integrity of this investigation. A discussion of statistical sampling would be worthwhile here. Discuss how to be random (rather than selective) in choosing items to measure. Or, ask your students to be certain to measure every item in a category—even that very long and skinny door in the kitchen cabinet that they hardly think of as a rectangle.

EXTENSION   Study rectangles found in packaging or advertising.

MORE INFORMATION   *Fascinating Fibonaccis,* chapter 3

ANSWERS   **1–10.** Students might find the golden ratio in the average of the ratios of the rectangles' dimensions, but not always. Conducting a statistically sound investigation and reflecting on the investigation are the main goals of the activity.

Rectangle Search

Examine rectangles on display in your home. Include examples such as posters, photographs, paintings, decorative rugs, and mirrors. Limit your investigation to decorations. You might limit your investigation simply to visible rectangles in your room.

For each rectangle, record the dimensions of its sides. Use a calculator to determine the ratio of the small side to the large side. Round to three decimal places.

Example: Length of small side is 34 cm and length of large side is 55 cm. The ratio is $\frac{34}{55}$ or 0.618.

1. Make a list on the back of this sheet of all the decimal ratios you find. How many do you have? _____

2. How many ratios are between 0.56 and 0.68? _____

3. What percent is this of the total? _____ % ($\frac{\text{answer 1}}{\text{answer 2}}$)

4. Find the average of all these ratios by adding them and then dividing the answer by the number of ratios. _____

5. Is this average between 0.56 and 0.68? _____

6. What is the difference between your average and 0.618? _____

7. Go through the above steps with any category of rectangles in your home.

   You might use

   • all the books on a certain shelf

   • all the greeting cards received on a recent holiday or birthday

   • all the magazines in a certain rack

   • all the catalogues that have accumulated

   • all the cabinet doors in your kitchen

   • all rectangular mirrors you can find

8. What percent of the ratios are between 0.56 and 0.68? _____ %

9. What is the difference between the average ratio and 0.618? _____

10. What conclusions can you make about the dimensions of the rectangles in your home?

TO THE TEACHER

Super Sleuth

CONNECTIONS	life science • field investigations
MATERIALS	copy of Project 3 chapter 2, *Fascinating Fibonaccis, Mystery and Magic in Numbers*
GROUPING	1 to 4
DURATION	See Notes
NOTES	Have students do this activity either as homework or as a group project over time.

Searching for Fibonacci numbers in the natural world is fascinating. Give students sufficient time to conduct these investigations and encourage them to do as many as interest them.

They need to understand chapter 2 of *Fascinating Fibonaccis, Mystery and Magic in Numbers*. This might be available in the classroom or the school library. Assign this reading in anticipation of this activity.

ALERT!

As exhilarating as it is to find Fibonacci numbers, it can be disappointing not to find them when you expect to.

Poor specimens of anything can be difficult to count, so students need to find good specimens. Pineapples often have an area on the surface that is difficult to count past. Sunflowers need to be dried (in seed form) to count. Sometimes Lucas numbers of spirals appear in sunflowers; on rare occasion there are double Fibonacci numbers of spirals (68 and 110 rather than 34 and 55, for example).

Some flowers resemble daisies. True daisies tend to exhibit Fibonacci numbers of petals, but not all flowers with petals are true daisies. Hybridizing seems to have an effect on Fibonacci numbers of anything, and it is not easy to tell if something has been hybridized.

Take heart, however, as there are lots and lots of Fibonacci numbers in your students' world.

EXTENSION

Rather than simply doing a report, put together an exhibit for the classroom or a display for the school.

MORE INFORMATION

Fascinating Fibonaccis, chapter 2

The Golden Section, chapter 11

NAME _____

Super Sleuth

To do this activity, you need to know how to find Fibonacci numbers in nature. Read chapter 2 (pages 6–18) of *Fascinating Fibonaccis: Mystery and Magic in Numbers.* Then choose one of the following investigations.

A. Examine growth spirals in plants such as pinecones, pineapples, artichokes, sunflowers, palm tree trunks, and branches (phyllotaxis).

B. Examine the numbers of petals in flowers. Be sure to examine several flowers to draw meaningful conclusions. You need to use both many of the same flower and many different types of flowers.

C. Examine the number of chambers (or sections) in fruits and vegetables. Again, consider many of the same fruit or vegetable and many different types of fruits and vegetables.

D. Search for Fibonacci numbers occurring naturally anywhere in the world around you. Look in the garden, park, country, mountains, desert, seashore, laboratory, sky at night, or anywhere else. You might be the first to find Fibonacci numbers where no one else has thought to look!

When you have completed your investigations, write a report about your findings. Include thefollowing:

- what you examined

- how many of those you examined

- what, if any, Fibonacci numbers or ratios you observed

- whether you found any Lucas numbers —1, 3, 4, 7, 11, 18, 29, 47, 76, . . . (a different sequence built the same way as Fibonacci numbers)

- your conclusion

Additional Ideas

Fibonacci numbers can liven up a classroom and pique students' curiosity while providing valuable lessons that are both varied and unifying. The following do not require activity sheets, but they are useful ideas. Many could be long-term, project-like assignments.

Fibonacci Food: Have a party featuring food characterized by Fibonacci numbers. For example, have cupcakes or cookies with Fibonacci numbers of candies on top. Serve fruit salad featuring fruit with Fibonacci numbers of chambers or segments such as apples, pears, bananas, persimmons, grapefruit, and melon. Give out Fibonacci proportions of any kind of fruit (55 grapes, 13 sliced plums, and so on). Virtually anything can be made with Fibonacci proportions of ingredients (2 c. sugar, 5 eggs, 1 stick of butter, 8 oz chocolate bits, 3 c. flour, and so on). How about 8 oz cheese melted over 34 tortilla chips served with 5 tbs. of salsa? Beyond the original suggestion, this party will need little teacher help.

Fibonacci Art: Encourage young artists to incorporate Fibonacci numbers into their work. They could feature the golden proportion in rectangles, triangles, or various divisions of space (such as the placement of fence posts or trees). They could also feature Fibonacci numbers of images— five sheep, eight people, three buildings, and so on.

Fibonacci Checkerboard Art: Mark off the sides of geometric shapes in sequential Fibonacci numbers of units. Then connect these markings in one of a variety of ways. The resulting grid has alternating units students can shade or color in a checkerboard fashion. There are many ways to do this, and the resulting patterns are interesting and attractive. Graph paper works well for this. Make overhead transparencies of the section openers on pages 11 and 57 and Supplement 5 on pages 70-71 for the class to see and discuss.

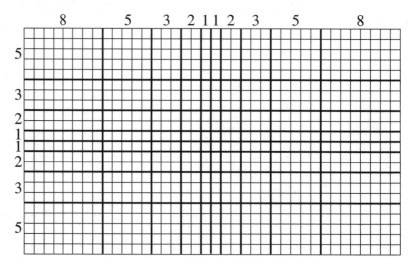

Fibonacci Music: Encourage young musicians to create a composition incorporating Fibonacci numbers or the golden proportion. Suggestions would include numbers of measures, numbers of half or whole steps between notes, and numbers of notes in the measures.

Fibonacci Crafts: Almost any craft item could incorporate Fibonacci numbers or the golden proportion. Beautiful sweaters have been made with horizontal stripes featuring the numbers or the ratio. Quilters can incorporate Fibonacci numbers in an infinite number of ways.

Fibonacci Sightings: Keep a running account of Fibonacci sightings. Do this regularly along the same vein as "show and tell" or current-events reports. Use a wall chart, index cards, or a newsletter to chronicle these sightings. These need not be limited to natural sightings, but could extend to design, architecture, music, poetry, and so on. For example, the picture on the wall in *Whistler's Mother* is a golden rectangle!

Science Fair Projects: Science fairs often have a mathematics category, though a project about Fibonacci numbers in nature could also fall into a biology or botany category. There is no end to the kinds of investigations and displays students could do using Fibonacci numbers or the golden proportion.

Mathematical Investigations: Mathematically inclined students should read chapter 7 of *Fascinating Fibonaccis, Mystery and Magic in Numbers* for an introduction to the mathematics of Fibonacci numbers. The Fibonacci Association has been carrying on such investigations for 30 years and publishes the *Fibonacci Quarterly* four times a year to share their findings. Gerald Bergum at South Dakota State University, Brookings, South Dakota 57007-1596, has been editor for some time.

Lucas numbers would also provide endless opportunities for investigation. Lucas numbers are the next most simple Fibonacci-type sequence; the first two numbers of the Lucas sequence are 1 and 3. Each subsequent number is the sum of the previous two numbers, just as with the Fibonacci sequence.

Tribonacci numbers begin 0, 1, 1, and each subsequent number is the sum of the previous three numbers. Students could investigate this sequence.

Tetranacci numbers begin 0, 0, 1, 1, and each subsequent number is the sum of the previous four numbers. These are sometimes called *quadranacci numbers*.

Students could also change Fibonacci's famous rabbit problem (see Activity 8). Perhaps a pair of rabbits needs two months to mature rather than one month. Perhaps each month, each adult pair could have two pairs of babies rather than one. What would happen then to the numbers? If Fibonacci had established different breeding rules for these rabbits, what might we now be calling Fibonacci numbers?

NAME _____

Crawling Critters

Use this sheet of mazes to trace paths from A up to and including I. Can you find as many different paths as you expect? Sketching them in an organized manner will help.

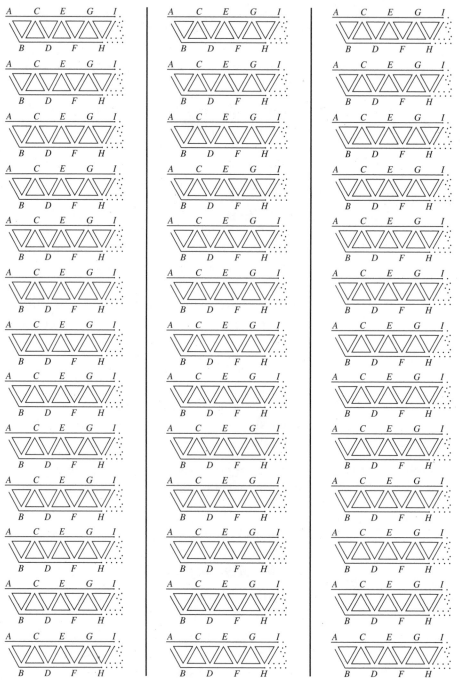

Pleasure Plotting

NAME _____

On a coordinate plane, plot the following points according to the numbered directions.

End means lift your pencil and begin again with the next numbered direction.
Remember, (4, 3) means 4 across and 3 up.

Connect (⁻10, ⁻10) to (⁻6, ⁻7). End.

Connect (⁻2, ⁻6) to (0, ⁻8) to (2, ⁻8) to (6, ⁻7)(⁻6. ⁻5). End.

Connect (1, 3) to (3, 3). End.

Connect (1, 2) to (2, $2\frac{1}{2}$) to (3, $2\frac{1}{2}$). End.

Connect (4, $\frac{-1}{2}$) to ($5\frac{1}{2}$, ⁻1) to (6, 0) to (5, 2) to ($5\frac{1}{2}$, 3) to ($6\frac{1}{2}$, 3). End.

Connect ($5\frac{1}{2}$, $2\frac{1}{2}$) to ($6\frac{1}{2}$, $2\frac{1}{2}$) End. 8.

Connect (3, ⁻$2\frac{1}{2}$) to (6, ⁻$2\frac{1}{2}$) to (5, ⁻3) to (4, ⁻3). End.

Connect the points in order starting at the top of each column.

(1, ⁻$4\frac{1}{2}$)	(⁻$5\frac{1}{2}$, 2)	(⁻5, 0)	(11, ⁻10)	(1, 10)
(3, ⁻$5\frac{1}{2}$)	(⁻7, ⁻1)	(⁻7, ⁻3)	(9, ⁻8)	(⁻2, 10)
(5, ⁻5)	(⁻7, ⁻3)	(⁻$7\frac{1}{2}$, ⁻4)	(6, ⁻7)	(⁻4, 8)
(6, ⁻3)	End	(⁻6, ⁻5)	(5, ⁻6)	(⁻4, 7)
(6, ⁻2)		(⁻$4\frac{1}{2}$, ⁻10)	(7, ⁻5)	(⁻6, 7)
(7, 0)		(⁻3, ⁻7)	(11, ⁻1)	(⁻7, 6)
($8\frac{1}{2}$, 0)		(⁻2, ⁻4)	(9, $3\frac{1}{2}$)	(⁻6, 3)
(9, $3\frac{1}{2}$)		(⁻3, ⁻3)	(10, 5)	End
(8, 6)		(⁻3, 0)	(9, 7)	(-2, $7\frac{1}{2}$)
(7, 6)		(⁻2, 3)	(7, 9)	(0, $7\frac{1}{2}$)
(6, 7)		(0, 5)	(4, 10)	(1, 8)
(3, $6\frac{1}{2}$)		(2, 6)	(1, 10)	(5, 8)
(1, 7)		(4, 6)	(⁻1, 9)	(9, 7)
(⁻2, 6)		(6, 5)	End	End
(⁻4, 7)		($7\frac{1}{2}$, 3)		
(⁻5, 4)		(7, 2)		
(⁻6, 3)		(7, 0)		
		End		

Center two small circles at (2, 2) and (6, 2). Fill in these circles, but leave a twinkle!

NAME _____

Tantalizing Triangles

Use these pentagons to help you find the golden triangles.

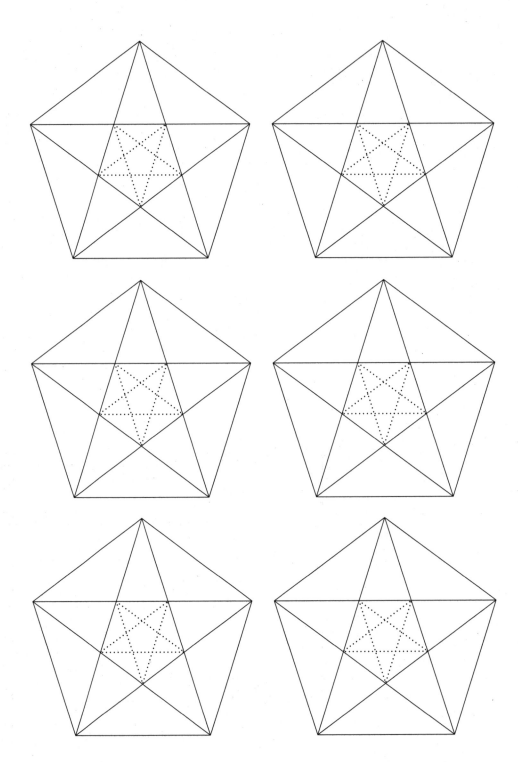

NAME _____

Fibonacci Mystery

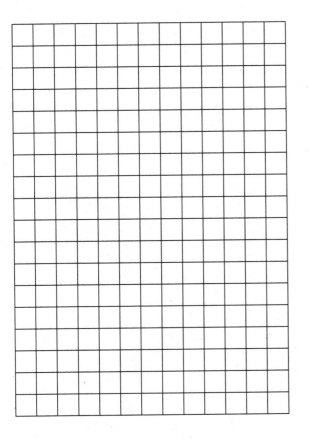

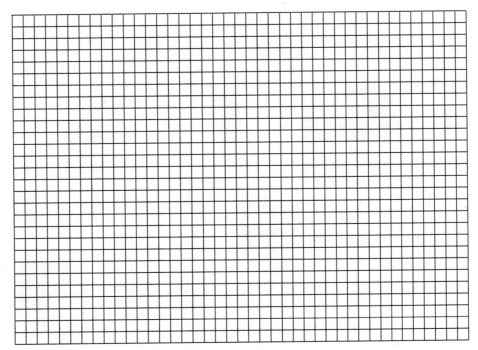

Fibonacci Art

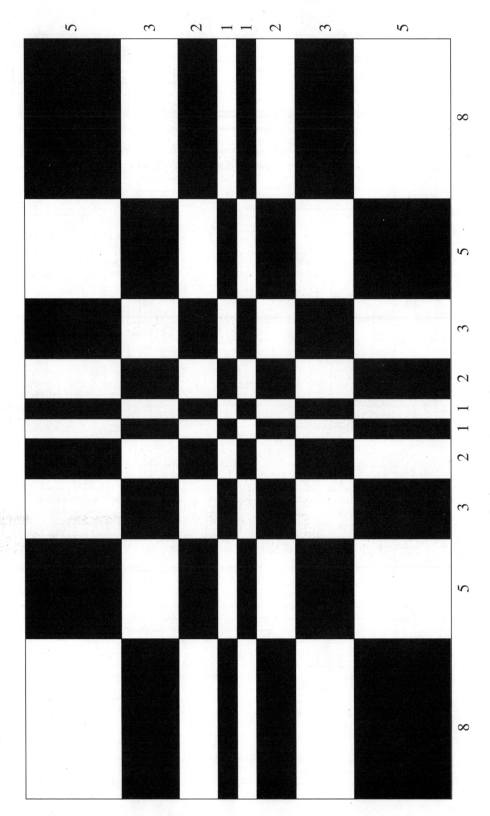

Glossary

converge *v.* To draw near to. A ratio converges to the golden ratio as the value of the ratio gets closer to 1.618.

frequency *adj. n.* For a collection of data, the number of items in a given category.

frequency histogram *n.* A graphic picture of a frequency distribution.

golden cut *n.* The division of a line segment AB by an interior point P so that $\frac{AB}{AP} = \frac{AP}{BP}$

golden section *n.* Another name for the golden cut.

golden proportion *n.* The relationship in which the ratio of one part to a larger part is the same as the ratio of the larger part to the whole. $\frac{A}{B} = \frac{B}{A+B}$

golden ratio *n.* The ratio 1.618. It is the ratio of the two sides of a golden rectangle or the two parts of a golden cut.

golden rectangle *n.* A rectangle with the property that it can be divided into a square and a new rectangle where the new rectangle is similar to the original rectangle. It's sides are related by the golden ratio.

proportion *n.* 1. (in mathematics) A statement of equality between two ratios. 2. (in art) The relation of parts to each another or to the whole.

ratio *n.* The comparison of two numbers by division.

recursive sequence *n.* A sequence whose definition includes the value of one or more initial terms and a formula that tells how to find each term from the previous terms.

similar *adj.* (in mathematics) Polygons with corresponding angles congruent and the lengths of corresponding sides in proportion. Two rectangles are similar if the ratios of the lengths of the sides of one rectangle is the same as the ratio of the lengths of the sides of the other.